# DRIFTING THROUGH
# ANCESTOR DREAMS

# DRIFTING THROUGH ANCESTOR DREAMS

New and Selected Poems
*by* Ramson Lomatewama

ENTRADA BOOKS
*A Division of Northland Publishing*

FIRST EDITION
ISBN 0-87358-552-6
Library of Congress Catalog Number 92-82838

Printed in the United States of America

Cover Design by David Jenney
Text Design by Rudy J. Ramos

Cataloging-in-Publication Data

Lomatewama, Ramson, 1953–
Drifting through ancestor dreams  :
new and selected poems  /  by Ramson Lomatewama.  —  1st ed.
74 p.   cm.
ISBN 0-87358-552-6  :  $9.95
1. Hopi Indians—Poetry.   I. Title.
PS3562.04664D7   1993
811'.54—dc20                            92-82838

3-92/1.5M/0425

# Contents

It Begins This Way

    It Begins This Way     3

    They Told Stories     5

    Evening Solitude     8

    Moments     10

    Dreams     11

    Moonlight     14

    Separation I     17

    Separation II     19

    In Our Home     20

    Resurrections     21

    At Edge     23

    Tuuwanasavi     24

    Life on the Road     27

    Untitled     29

    Mare Futurus     33

    Offerings     35

    Eagles     38

    Drifting Through Ancestor Dreams     41

Silent Winds

    A Casual Acquaintance     45

    A Rain Song     46

    Ants     47

After the Rains     48

Cloud Brothers     50


Ascending the Reed

    Birth     55

    Blue Flute Spring     56

    Song to the Breeze     59

    Barren     60

    Lovescape     62

    Last Song     65


About the Author     68

# It Begins This Way
*(on composing poetry)*

"How do I compose poetry?"

It begins this way

I guess/I just start composing/when I think of life/I think about my
children/other people/nature/prayers/our hopes/and disillusions/
everything/and anything/all people/especially those I know

When I think of life/I see poetry/but I think in song/I look at tradition/art/
language/life/what we do/our lives/the things that sustain us/planting/
singing/praying

I like to think of purpose/long life/prosperity/happiness/beauty/purity/
balance in all things/These thoughts come anytime/anyplace

When I ponder sunsets/when I'm driving that lonely stretch of road/or when
I'm alone/especially when I'm by myself/I think best then

After a time/minutes/maybe months/I start to hear their song/barely at
first/then it starts happening/it crystallizes/and then I hear music/and words
begin to form/I don't know how it happens/it just does/but you have to have
patience/you can't rush nature

It comes/sometimes in trickles/sometimes in floods/I just keep singing to myself/saying words/phrases/over and over/I sing at sunrise/or when I carve/I sing when I plant corn/when I watch hummingbirds/I see everything around me in song

I keep singing/until music and words come together/it's creativity and prayer/they come together/and when it's right/you know/your heart tells you/and then you sing it to yourself/out loud/and when it's done/your heart knows

You feel good inside/happy/and when they tell you/you sing your poem to others

I don't know exactly/what moves me to compose/or from what source these poems come/but one thing I know for sure/you pray/and ask those who live unseen/to reveal and share their songs/their designs/and you give thanks

as long as I have faith in life/I will continue to compose

I believe that is how it happens.

# They Told Stories

They told stories
with rough hands
and drops of sweat,
sharing with us
fragments of their journeys
pecked into sandstone walls.

I follow their footsteps
as my fingers gently follow
every curve,
every worn line—
feeling another time,
finding warmth in ancient spirals
and lightning of those
who left long ago.

I stand alone
and feel their faces,
frozen in centuries of seasons.
I gaze deep into their mottled eyes
remembering words handed down,
tracing with my fingers each and every antelope;
following migration patterns chipped into memories;

looking for songs in snakes and water waves;
letting upraised arms of ancestor spirits
hold my numbed hands.

I follow their journey in stone
from our third world,
reaching hand over hand,
ascending the reed;
coming into canyons,
reaching higher and higher
like sprouted corn
stretching upward to light.
I feel their words
and hear echoes of past lives.

I brace myself, breathing hard and steady.
I stay to drink every drop of their grit-filled stories,
taking in every moment,
every image of who I am,
before winter's jagged wind
drives me from this place.

# Evening Solitude

Drop by drop
Rainbow appears
and dances with butterfly maidens.

They flutter above
tassels of red corn
gliding on windy fingers of spring.

Crows upon crows
polish their silver-black flight
on Taawa's turquoise road
circling higher and higher
until they cross Moon's first light.

I sift warm sand between my fingers
rest on your blanket of cool shade
listen to cottonwood showering music
into my long, flowing hair.

I breathe Cricket's evening song
reach up to feel Night's desire

dance down with stars

falling silently
into Owl's midnight call.


*Taawa: Sun*

# Moments

When you spun around
summer light played with your smooth hair

And that smile

the one you shared
when you gazed in wonder at butterflies emerging

was just as beautiful.

# Dreams

In planting corn moon
I heard rising waves
rippling outward
above tangled grass.

You and I gathered my seeds . . .
gathered them tenderly
in your lovely woven basket.

We sat above blue-gray clouds
watching infinite fields of dark water.

You cupped your cool hands under my chin
and made me smile . . .
waved my long black hair
towards red flowered hills.

I asked you in whispers that came from afar,
"Can you feel pulsing stars in my eyes,
when I gaze into midnight?"

"Do you feel as I feel now,
being everything . . . and nothing?"

I listened, but did not hear your voice.
Only your soft breath and your warmth.

Was it then
that shadows of blue lightning
danced below us
and we finally knew?

Or was it
when we drifted
far over red horizons
to that beginning

where we too
became ashes
and no more?

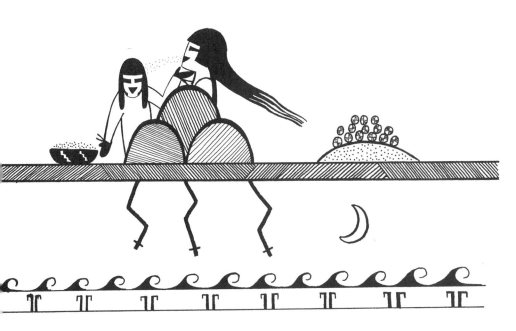

# Moonlight

Bright and full
high above ice-covered pond

her smooth reflection
floats feather-light

Slowly
I wander with her
following her glitter-laced path

We reach my home
letting gray light cascade
to melt in blue snow

My eyes dance
with soft shadows
of snow maiden's breath

Gazing upon moonlight
through frosted windows
I wait

and listen for voices

in trails of fading clouds

Night after night
I fall asleep

In my dreams
Owl ponders her final silver crescent
and I watch her slowly fade away.

## Separation I

Together
we lay arm in arm
breathing softly
your sleep—our child.

High above
stars surrender one by one
like autumn leaves that die
and fall to earth.

Far below
Muyingwa rests
among buttercup blossoms
dreaming and singing new songs to life.

Beyond our window
clouds of coral
rest upon warm breasts of dawn.

Beyond our window
on dawn's other side
snow children caress our love.

I feel quiet rain
trickling down our warm and blossom-laced thighs
trickling down our soft autumn skin
trickling down our tender light of crescent moon.

At morning
smooth wings of sparrows
flutter and glide
in never-ending flute music patterns.

Before too long
one must leave
to chase butterflies and rain.

# Separation II

I leave you behind
to ponder my past.

I walk down worn trails in silence
lay down hooma and greet Taawa
who looks upon my every step
now embraced in snowcrust.

I whisper words only they can hear
I reach toward morning
not with my arms
but with my heart.

Behind me
she longs to caress one more day.

Alone again
I become only shadow
lost
under reign of fading stars

missing you.

*Hooma: White cornmeal*

# In Our Home

Gray skies
low clouds
wet snow

shifting wind
sandstone walls
orange light

warm stove
scent of cedar
quiet hearts

crackling fire
sleeping child
You and I

# Resurrections

We hit it off in no time
you and I.

Taking stabs
at politicians and mothers
and things we love
under suns and moons.

For hours
we made watery circles
on small round tables.
Peeled labels off bottled beer.
Filled ashtrays with offerings
of our almost forgotten childhoods.

All night long
those neon lights hummed
and turned our lips electric blue.
Friday's dance floor churned warm sweat
and smoke-filled time
swirled with our many lives
reborn again and again
with each and every breath.

That night
memories became flesh.
Confessions crawled out with every round.
Slurred philosophies dangled
like black widows on delicate threads.

When

will our morning come?

## At Edge

I lie with pearl beach
sinking skin deep
leaving dreams of abalone
and coral far behind.

I wait
and watch dying stars fall
thinking in circles
with distant lighthouse
spinning silent gray
cutting through fog and mist
coming full circle
lighting ways
for nameless ships
as they break water
sailing farther away

until
only black smoke
is visible.

# Tuuwanasavi

Two purple blades of grass
stood at Tuuwanasavi.
Cracked asphalt
ran beyond four directions.

One stood alone
caught by rain
having less
than a pocketful of change.

I watched him
digging in his dumpster
in his alley
below my easy chair.

His eyes were lost in light.
His hands trembled
when he wiped steamy sweat my way.

He sat down
and leaned against his bedroll
stained with endless nights
against our garbage bin

in loving ways.

At noon
he swept away empty boxes
searched for bits of luxury
fished for cans that he could trade for coins
or maybe
long lost friends.

At Tuuwanasavi
they stood alone

invisible

like distant stars
whose radiance
we
do not know.

# Life on the Road

After Suzy died
they let her stay around
till day's first light.

Blankly she stared
wide-eyed
like calm desert sky.

No one knew exactly when
or why she gave her last.
Only her world knows.

We can only guess
can't we?
I could.

You see
I've come across cows
bloated along lonely black roads.

Many times.

If Suzy is lucky,

her family will take her home
and bury her at noon.

Let earth take in Suzy.
Let buzzards take in cows.
Let all things

come full circle.

# Untitled
*(for my uncles)*


You became rain-laden
like you said you would.
This morning, I heard your song
when clouds dark and pregnant with rain
appeared in great swells over Nuvatukya'ovi.

I listened to your rain song
dancing down, brushing our mother's soft skin.
I pondered your beautiful black hair
descending along distant red cliffs
that Tobacco Clan people say is their Eagle womb.

Now, I watch as you turn away from Sun's journey,
toward tomorrow, where you said you would go.

At last, we come together
and follow our delicate paths
meeting dawn halfway.
I follow your footsteps in patters of rain—
I hear you whisper
"Aqwhaqami siìtala, oovi uma umuùqatsiy ööqalyani."

All around
my children stand quiet and still,
their golden tassels flowing into themselves.
We listen to their evening laughter.

Together
we shall create beauty
and share what is.

Everything.

Now
and beyond all we imagine . . .

beyond unborn songs.

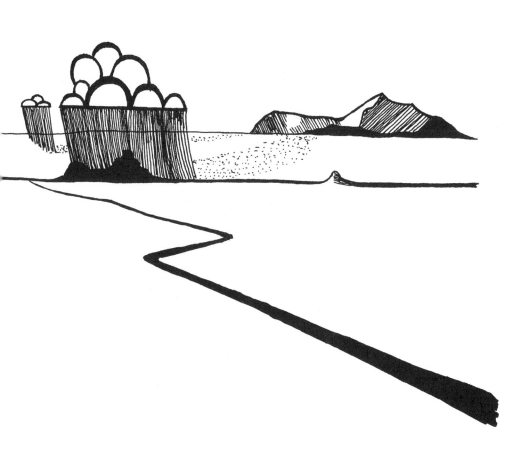

## Mare Futurus

I return
to hear your rhythmic voice
swaying back and forth,
soothing me.

I stand
and slowly sink
as your wet silver hair rushes
to caress my feet.

Do you remember me,
standing here many years ago,
watching your frothy white waves
pulsing with Moon's pale crescent?

Do you remember that time
when So-oh,
still wearing her calico apron,
knelt beside your vastness
in awe?

And I took with me
brightly colored shells and memories?

But for some unknown reason,
little by little
those years became fluid like you,
and such that I could no longer hold them
together.

Now,
I look upon empty and broken shells
making their way back
to Paatuuwaqatsi.

One day,
they may return brightly colored—
if not for me,
then
for my children.

*So-oh: Grandmother*
*Paatuuwaqatsi: Ocean*

# Offerings

We wait for tomorrow
sitting in darkness,
feeling warmth of coal burning.

Moon's light reflects sparkling snow
and enters our home through windows.

And slowly,
shadows change with each breath
as Moon travels across night's field of stars.

I sit alone
and remember white walls
yellowed and parched,
barely holding on to faded colors.

I see you still
clearly,
as if it was I
who painted clouds and rain upon your sides,
and filled you with hooma,
and dressed you with offerings.

I look back
wondering whose hands gathered colors
to paint thoughts and prayers,
whose heart was to be touched,
whose memory was to be carried forth.

As I watch dawn's purple light,

I hear earth's heartbeat.

I hear tomorrow's blossom.

I hear purity in homes underground.

I hear grains of sand shifting into spring.

I hear his song blending with mine.

I hear his offering blending with mine.

# Eagles

This morning, I watch gray fog
snake its way along frozen meadows
glistening with snow.

Pastel red clouds hover
over pine-covered mountains
stretching eastward, silently.

Driving along this snow-covered road,
I watch Moon's fading light
descending behind Nuvatukya'ovi.

I look upward above empty white fields
and ponder eagles soaring higher and higher
in circles never-ending, as life itself.

# Drifting Through Ancestor Dreams


They come from all sides, these words and songs of ancestors.
They slide out on tongues of Felipe Molina, flowers, and deer,
and from spruce trees, long houses, and Joe Bruchac.
They fly at me across deserts, from summer stars over Awatovi,
and from bottomless silver words of Mike Kabotie.
I see their words are made of bamboo, tradition, and myth,
and images of Jung and Campbell, and long ago walks in cornfields.
They find me and speak to me through memories of Chicago streets,
Lee Young Lee, Sybil Dunbar, and Ofelia Zepeda's jagged mountains.
Their words and songs come through dreams of Rex Jim and Harold
Littlebird, whose poems, words, and drumbeats dance all around.
They whisper in flights of hummingbirds and high mesas, through
Luci Tapahanso and Shiprock, and through journeys of Simon Ortiz.
Ancestor dreams come to me from your world, from dark skies,
from unborn children, from New Delhi and from Tuuwanasavi.
I dream-travel through ancestor songs; dream over eagle feathers
dipped in honey and rain; around summer clouds and roasted corn.
I journey with you, creating abstractions and simple songs.
I listen for ancestor songs in all people and all places.
I am drifting through ancestor dreams,
drifting
to my final breath.

*Silent Winds*

# A Casual Acquaintance

I'm struggling to
carry an armload
of sweet
fresh
corn . . . still moist
from the last rain.

A bullsnake
taking refuge
curled around
the coolness
of a
strong
corn plant.

Our eyes meet.
I walk past.
Neither of us says
"hello."

45

# A Rain Song

blue butterfly maiden
yellow butterfly maiden

they chase one another through the cornfield
they chase one another throughout the day

they are happy

from the west
the rain will come

from the east
the rain will come

blue corn maiden
yellow corn maiden

they grow throughout the cornfield
they grow throughout the day

they are happy

# Ants

Silence is reflected upon the sky
for the blue haze is but a mirror.

I can feel
the subtleness of the breeze
and the silent fluttering of the moth.

A field of tall grass
sends a gentle wave of light
across the land.

It flows to eternity. 47

I gaze upon the ants
who toil for their children

for they do not consider
the lilies of the field.

## After the Rains

Sandstone cliffs
reflect the red
of the setting sun.

My hoe is caked
with evidence
of my labor.

I see clouds
going to the east.
Dark clouds.

I look to the sky.
There!
A rainbow
is arched above me.

As I walk down
the dusty road
I look up.

Again!
The rainbow

dressed in beauty
walks with me.

There is no need
for us to speak.

Silence
will speak
for us.

# Cloud Brothers

Four directions
cloud brothers
share one sky.

      Each has its own path.

      Each has its own mood.

      Each has its own face.

The cloud brothers are many
but they are one family.

The cloud brothers are scattered
but they are one spirit.

They mingle
within themselves

changing with every moment.

They tell us
that we too
are brothers

on this land.

And

like our cloud brothers

we are all yellow
       as are the sunrise clouds

we are all white
       as are the noonday clouds

we are all black
       as are the thunder clouds

we are all red
       as are the sunset clouds.

So let us look up to our cloud brothers
as one family
and one spirit.

For we       are truly different

and yet

    we       are truly the same.

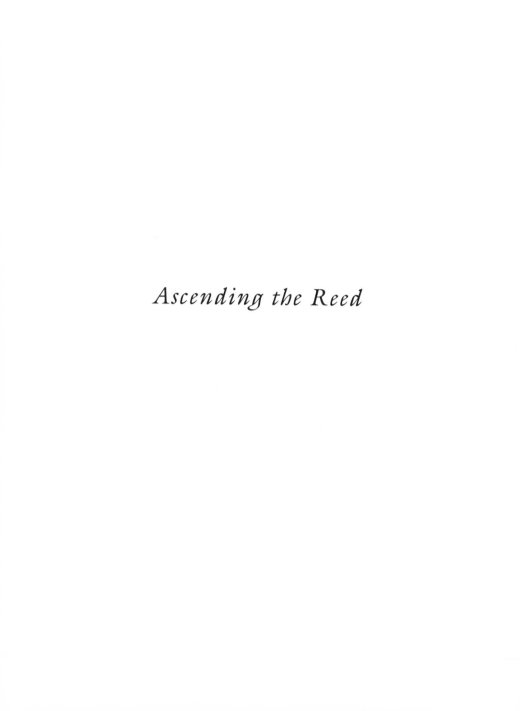

*Ascending the Reed*

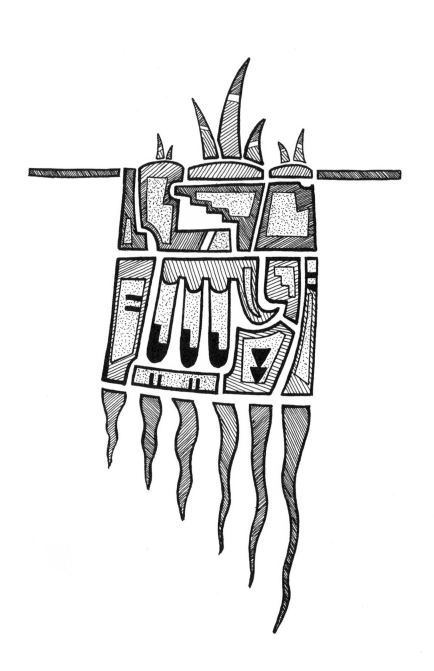

# Birth

Young corn breaks ground
showered by rays of the rising sun.

They grow in happiness,
become filled with warmth.

Silky tassels grow long,
like my hair,
in search of new beginnings.

Tomorrow,
itaha taawa
travels the longest day.

With pipe in hand,
we await our elders
who bring rain.


*Itaha taawa: My uncle, the sun*

## Blue Flute Spring

Shallow clear water
falling stars
reflected on ripples
tails of fire
burnished into life                        forever.

Soft green moss
dance along banks
at Blue Flute Spring
swaying
ever so gently.

Drops of rain
make widening circles,
they interweave
and fade into silence.

Paa-atu, the water spider,
rides reflection
of August full moon.
Stars are looking down                        pondering.

Crickets and frogs

gather at water's edge
singing songs of joy.

Desert Rose
listens with me
as Gray-mist Woman
dances
with harvest night.

Velvet shadows lie
with Blue Flute stones
that rest
and sleep under stream.

Spider Woman comes
and listens to chanting water.
Heartbeats echo                    within.

I listen
as Firefly Maiden
sings light
among Sumac People.

I listen as Thundercloud Fathers
travel from mountain kivas
melting all darkness
with lightning.

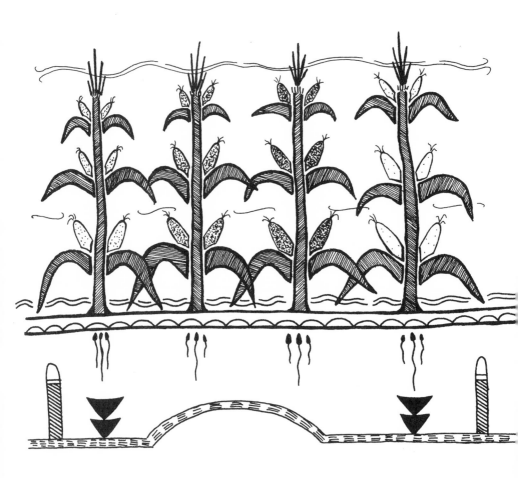

# Song to the Breeze

When you whisper
to four-color corn,
they laugh.
You make them laugh.
We walk among corn children,
caressing tender young leaves.
We help corn maidens
tease the ground,
tickle the earth
when their leaves,
green and slender,
stroke the sleeping sand.
Sand laughs
and swirls away.
You help the sand run away.
You watch me laugh
when I hear them laugh.
My song to you
is filled with laughter.
Can you hear the song?
Do you feel the song?
Can you hear?
Can you hear?

# Barren

Under the rolling hills,
a grave of silent crickets
turns away from
the wandering soul.
Stars appear
one by one.
Our mother
turned barren
with the coming of Kyaamuya.
Tonight, the moon hides her face.
A man and a woman
walk hand in hand,
reflecting the past
with tears and whispers.
The dark trail
leads to the home of ants;
there is no life within.
Tonight,
a wandering bear child
bleeds at the paws.
Far to the north,
a desperate pack of stray dogs
trample the graves

that lie under the rolling hills.
A home atop the mesa
is barren.
Tonight,
the streets of Delhi
are trampled by the millions.

# Lovescape

Brittle summer evening,
cliffs and canyons
scorched by crimson sky.
Darkness becomes master.
I gaze into mystery fire.
My soul melts
becoming cloistered
in dancing flames.
And after time unknown
my eyes drink
the glowing embers.

It was then
that I saw her,
bathing in fires
of all time.
She pondered antiquity,
and dust of her memories
stirred once more
and turned to streaks of lightning.
Then
with beauty of life
she spoke to the night

and me.
"I am the daughter of nature
and I reflect intense desires
of you
and me."
My eyes
and the blue-gray light
of the weeping moon
stroked her soft and tender face.
She smiled
not at me,
but at the lonely moon.
She consoled the moon
with her smile,
and I fell deeper and deeper
in love.

Brittle summer morning
cliffs and canyons
soothed by crimson sky.
Dawn becomes master.
Splinters of burnt offerings
lay about
like shattered pottery.
I held the future in my hands.
Last night

I was so close to you
I watched your eyes
dance with stars.

I watched you
caress the lonely moon.
I heard the comfort
of your celestial heart.
I felt your breath
running with mine.
And when you spoke to me in the night,
stars watched.
All universe ceased to exist,
except you

and I
together.

# Last Song

Life dances
in the womb
of our village.

Spirits of long ago
sing on purified sand.

The songs of beauty and life
seep down into the earth.

Rattling down the rain,
they sing of happiness.

Gourds of thunder
rumble under the song.

They dance one final prayer.
It is time for the last song.

Somewhere far away,
Spruce Tree People
listen for rain songs.

Somewhere far away,
white clouds and rainbows
listen for one final prayer.

And here,
people of the fourth world
listen for the last song.

It is here
that we part with the breaking of branches.

# About the Author

RAMSON LOMATEWAMA, artist, writer, and educator, was born into the Eagle Clan in 1953. His life on the Hopi Reservation is clearly the heart of his poetry, and his way of looking at the world is a reflection of his rich heritage and the timeless culture of the Hopi people.

He has published two previous books of poetry, *Silent Winds: Poetry of One Hopi* and *Ascending the Reed*. Ramson is also a freelance writer, having published poems and articles for numerous publications and magazines.

Since September 1991, Ramson has been spending more time with his stained glass work. However, he still involves himself with painting, carving kachina dolls, and writing. On occasion, he travels widely as a consultant in the areas of creative writing and cultural anthropology.

Ramson and his family currently live on their five acre farm just outside Flagstaff, Arizona. They still return to their native land whenever possible.